gaia **organic** basics

weeds

Charlie Ryrie

Gaia Books Ltd

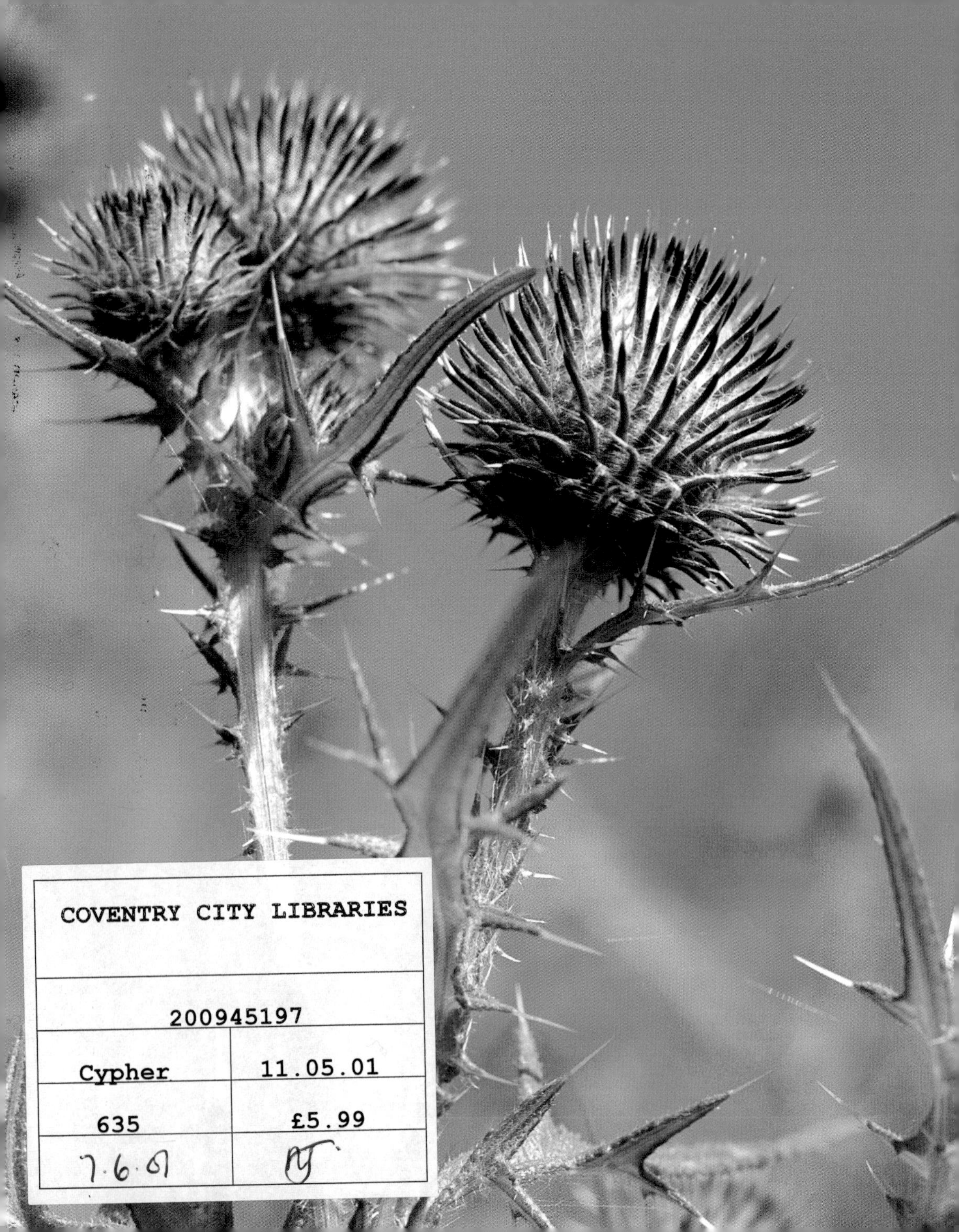

CONTENTS

PREFACE

Soil Association

The membership charity
campaigning for an organic Britain

Organic growers and gardeners all know that there are many different approaches to weed control. An important part of the strategy is to increase understanding of the way in which these plants spread and survive. They are all part of the bigger picture that is revealed when an organic system is introduced.

Weeds, for all their faults, can be very useful in many ways by mining for trace elements, providing compost material, encouraging beneficial insects and sometimes for their natural beauty. They can be eaten, used as a living mulch, for green manure and so are not always the nuisance we imagine. Very few of the weeds we encounter will actually prevent our flowers and vegetables from growing and, at worst, can be considered unsightly.

Whether you want a weed-free garden or are prepared to allow a certain level of invasion, organic controls are cost effective, harmless to the environment and will provide a surprising insight into the way your garden works. This book explains in an uncomplicated way how to appreciate the value of weeds and helps us to understand their place in the garden. Practical methods of weed control are not as daunting as we might believe and the advice given here is simple and effective.

Rob Hayward
Horticultural Development Officer
The Soil Association

Weeds are sometimes described as being the wrong plant in the wrong place. How true! The sort of gardener who loves their lawn looking like a billiard table doesn't appreciate patches of moss spoiling the effect, but a more relaxed gardener dotes on daisies and buttercups.

Organic gardeners value weeds as much as they despair of them, as this book describes so well. Weeds can help to cover otherwise bare soil and protect it from the weather. Those with long tap roots can bring up valuable nutrients from deep in the soil to feed another generation of crops. Weeds are also useful indicators of the type of soil they grow in. And don't forget, you can eat and enjoy many common garden weeds.

However, some weeds just have to go and this book describes a host of chemical-free ways of getting rid of them. For example, mulching the soil with materials like straw or leafmould is a technique which can look most attractive. Perhaps the most important thing to decide is what level of weediness you are happy to live with.

HDRA, the organic organisation, is one of the oldest environmental organisations. It researches, promotes and advises on organic cultivation for home gardeners everywhere. It works to continually improve composting, pest and disease control and other techniques, to enable organic gardeners to produce better crops of sturdy, healthy vegetables, fruits and ornamentals.

Jackie Gear
Executive Director
HDRA, the organic organisation

the organic
organisation

An international membership organisation, researching and promoting organic horticulture and agriculture

WHY

SHOULD I KNOW MY WEEDS?

Just because weeds are usually uninvited, this doesn't always mean they should always be unwelcome in your garden. Don't be too hasty to uproot them all as they are nature's way of colonising bare ground and some can help both garden and gardener.

WHY SHOULD I KNOW MY WEEDS?

As weeds are rarely deliberately invited into our gardens, they are usually unwanted, but this doesn't mean they are all undesirable. Some may turn out to be useful to garden and gardener. There are dozens of definitions of weeds, from 'plants growing in the wrong place' to 'plants whose virtues have not yet been discovered'.

Some weeds are troublesome: they may host pests and diseases; they can smother your chosen plants; they will certainly compete for food, moisture and light, and crowd out plants that you do want. They often interfere with the way that we may wish to use a particular area of land, but they are not all bad. Get to know your weeds, using this book with a reliable identification guide. Once you appreciate their better qualities you will be more tolerant of them, and able to spend less time weeding and more time enjoying other aspects of gardening.

Invaders

We tend to think of weeds as some kind of superplants that invade our gardens without our say-so and take over. But in fact weeds only flourish when we make a place for them. A thriving well-managed garden will have few places for weeds as their job is to colonise bare land and open soil, to bring stability to disturbed sites so that no earth is left uncovered. They are one of nature's strategies for protecting bare soil and preventing erosion. When we cultivate the soil in our gardens we create an ideal environment for most weeds to get stuck in.

Just like the plants we do choose, weeds also need particular soil and climate conditions. Unfortunately, they often like similar conditions to crop plants, and weeds are usually stronger – after all, they have survived for generations with only incidental help. Horsetail apparently existed in Jurassic times. But, like cultivated plants, there are some conditions weeds don't enjoy, and once you realise how they operate you can get rid of them.

Garden helpers

Weeds do have good points: deep-rooted weeds such as dock, fat hen, and even the humble dandelion mine deep into the soil for minerals not available in the upper layers of soil. Handweed and compost the dandelions to return these minerals to your soil.

Wild grasses often have such persistent root systems that they break up compacted soil and improve its structure. Others may provide homes to helpful insects that help control the pests in your garden.

Most weeds provide fodder for animals, and many are edible for humans as well – common weeds such as nettles and dandelions are delicious as well as more nutritious than many cultivated vegetables. a number of wild plants and weeds contain substances that are now recognised as useful in conventional as well as herbal medicine. Many more are waiting to be discovered.

Control

When you garden organically, you are gardening with nature as much as possible. But you still want control over what grows in your garden. You may appreciate a colony of coltsfoot or rosebay willowherb as a beautiful patch of wildflowers in an open field; the white trumpet flowers of bindweed look glorious clambering over hedges or up trees. But they can become rampant in your garden.

A few weeds are poisonous, and others are home to all sorts of pests and diseases. Some weeds are a nuisance and you will need to find ways to discourage or eradicate them. Fortunately, there are plenty of effective organic techniques for weed control. On the other hand, some weeds actually help to keep garden and gardener healthy. So before you rush to discover ways to uproot them all, always remember that some plants that are seen as weeds are actually useful additions to your garden.

• Biennials
  Burdock *Arctium lappa*
  Garlic mustard *Alliaria petiolata*
  Ragwort *Senecio jacobaea*
  Teasel *Dipsacus fullonum*

• Perennials
  Bindweed *Convolvulus arvensis*
  Bracken *Pteridium aquilinum*
  Coltsfoot *Tussilago farfara*
  Comfrey *Symphytum officinale*
  Couch grass *Agropyron repens*
  Cow parsley *Anthriscus sylvestris*
  Creeping buttercup *Ranunculus repens*
  Creeping cinquefoil *Potentilla repens*
  Creeping thistle *Cirsium arvense*
  Dandelion *Taraxacum officinale*
  Dock *Rumex spp.*
  Field garlic *Allium vineale*
  Greater celandine *Chelidonium majus*
  Ground elder *Aegopodium podagraria*
  Ground ivy *Glechoma hederacea*
  Hedge bindweed *Calystegia sepium*
  Horsetail *Equisetum arvensis*
  Ivy *Hedera helix*
  Lesser Celandine *Ranunculus ficaria*
  Nettle *Urtica dioica*
  Oxalis *Oxalis articulata*
  Plantain *Plantago major*
  Rosebay willowherb *Epilobium angustifolium*
  Selfheal *Prunella vulgaris*
  Silverweed *Potentilla anserina*
  Toadflax *Linaria vulgaris*
  White deadnettle *Lamium album*
  Yarrow *Achillea millefolium*

WHAT

USE ARE WEEDS?

Weeds can tell you about
your soil and may even help
to improve or stabilise it.
They make nutritious
compost, they can attract
helpful creatures, they may
be edible, or they may help
the health of garden or
gardener.

WEEDS AS SOIL INDICATORS

When you take over a new patch of ground the first thing you'll want to know is what kind of soil you're dealing with. Before you lift a spade, take a look at what's growing, as the resident weeds can give you a good idea of the kind of soil you're dealing with. If your weed population is very varied, your soil is probably reasonably fertile, but where certain weeds predominate, it will be because your soil provides their favourite environment. As weeds are greedy colonisers and will try any soil rather than none, looking at weeds can never be 100 per cent accurate, but it's a good start.

Plants have to get all their food from the soil, which needs to contain a balanced diet for them to thrive. The most important elements are nitrogen (N), phosphorus (P) and potassium (K). Calcium levels are crucial and magnesium and sulphur are also vital. Then plants also need trace elements in smaller quantities, including iron, magnesium, boron, zinc, copper and molybdenum. As adequate nitrogen is vital for strong and leafy growth, nitrogen has the most obvious effect on your plants. The level of calcium, or pH level, is also vital as this affects the ability of plants to access the other elements in your soil.

When your soil lacks certain nutrients, the plants that are most successful at seeking them out will flourish. Learn what conditions weeds prefer, and their presence can indicate your soil's strengths and deficiences.

Indicator plants
Some plants are able to fix nitrogen from the air as well as the soil, so they will flourish if the soil is particularly low in this essential element. These are legumes, members of the pea and bean family, including vetches, clovers and black medick. If your garden is full of weed legumes it's actually quite a good sign, as they will be putting nitrogen back into the soil so that future plants will benefit from it.

Acid soil

Many weeds will thrive in mineral-deficient soil. Sorrel is often used as an indicator that soil is acid, lacking calcium and needs lime or seaweed to increase its pH to a level where most plants will flourish. However, although sorrel will grow happily in poor acidic soil, it will also grow in more fertile soil if that's all that's available. You can get a good clue from how sorrel tastes: it becomes increasingly bitter the more acid the soil it grows in. Corn spurrey is a more reliable indicator as it tolerates extremely acid conditions.

Knotgrass is common in acidic sandy soils. Plantain grows best in acidic soils, whereas dandelions are often pale and stunted. Horsetail tells you that your land is not only rather acid, but also poorly drained.

Alkaline soil

Field pansies, charlock and wild poppies on the other hand thrive in more alkaline soil. So be sure to add plenty of compost when you cultivate the soil to lower the pH to near neutral, where most cultivated plants will thrive.

Fertile soil

Where chickweed and groundsel flourish, the soil is generally well-structured and fertile – and they are easy weeds to uproot if you want to get rid of them. Cleavers, speedwell and fumitory also imply that the soil contains plenty of available food, while nettles, dock, sowthistle and fat hen suggest high levels of available nitrogen.

As your garden becomes more fertile, weeds will be less and less keen to live there. But if the annual crop of summer weeds increases year on year this indicates declining fertility, so test the pH and add, if necessary, plenty of compost and manure to your soil.

MATCHING WEED TO SOIL

Fertile soils
chickweed
nettle
cleavers
deadnettle
borage
speedwell
redshank
sun spurge
creeping thistle
fumitory
sowthistle
stinging nettle
dandelion
groundsel

Acid soils
corn spurrey
sorrel
plantain
knotgrass

Alkaline soils
field pansy
field mouse ear
poppy
charlock

Generally poor soils
poppies
dock

Compacted soils
grasses
greater plantain
pineapple mayweed
silverweed

Too much nitrogen
cow parsley

Too little nitrogen
vetches
clovers
medick

Poorly drained soils
horsetail
creeping buttercup
silverweed
coltsfoot
dock
ragged robin
butterwort
bog pimpernel
sedges
mosses

WHAT DO WEEDS DO FOR MY SOIL?

Many weeds have the advantages of being sturdier and more deep-rooted than their cultivated companions. While this can be irritating in borders and beds where they are competing for resources with cultivated plants, it is extremely useful in poor and bare soils.

Preventing soil erosion
When you leave any patch of soil bare, the weather will work at it to destroy the structure, and wash or blow away the nutrients plants need. When rain falls onto bare clay soil it causes puddling, or areas where water gathers without draining away. This compacts the soil so air can't get into it, and water can't drain through it and it becomes increasingly infertile – the more compacted the soil structure, the less nutrition can get in or out of the soil. When rain falls onto bare sandy soil it washes the top layers away, sometimes exposing the subsoil where top-soil layers are thin. Even the best loam soils suffer from weathering if they are left bare.

Weeds naturally gravitate to bare soil. They want to use any that they can find, if they possibly can – you know you have serious problems if weeds do not take it over as this suggests your soil is not in a condition where even the toughest plants are tempted to live.

As they cover the ground, their roots help to improve both the structure of the soil and the nutrition within it. Weeds are opportunists – they are used to digging around to find what they need, unlike most cultivated plants which expect their needs to be catered for. If what they need isn't immediately available, they search for it. This is why some weeds have such well-developed branching roots, giving them the best chance of finding the food they need, whatever the condition of the soil.

The root systems of many grasses, including the detested couch grass, can travel many metres, with no respect for other plants that might get in their way: if you grow root vegetables in a plot infested with couch grass don't be surprised to dig up your crop to find couch grass roots growing right through them.

But this isn't all bad news. If you have to leave a patch of couch grass for a year or so before attending to it, it will have spread dramatically and take longer to remove, but as it spreads it leaves hundreds of fine channels in the soil, where its roots ran. So it leaves the soil better aerated and therefore with improved drainage, particularly in a heavy soil.

Don't weed – increase fertility

Organic gardeners often grow green manure, a cover crop of plants grown to be dug into the soil rather than harvested. They are sown expressly to prevent leaving soil bare, and to increase fertility when they are incorporated into the soil. When the crop is mature, and before it flowers, dig it in to the ground or cut and leave it on top of the soil as a mulch.

Annual weeds can fulfil the same purpose if you don't have time to clear the ground and sow green manure. Treat them in the same way as any cover crop – never let them flower and set seed or you will increase your problems immeasurably. While growth is fairly lush cut them down and fork them into the top few centimetres of soil. Then you are preventing erosion, adding nutrition to the soil through the nutrients the plants will have stored in their leaves and stems, and adding organic matter to the soil to increase the activity of soil life. Or you can cut and compost them.

If clovers, vetches or black medick colonise areas of your garden, even in flower and vegetable beds, leave them in the ground for as long as you can, as they increase available nitrogen in your soil. When you weed them out, leave them on the surface for earthworms and other soil organisms to incorporate them into the soil.

THE BENEFITS OF DEEP FEEDERS

As you cultivate your garden horsetail will gradually disappear because it won't survive in very fertile soil. It is an interesting and ancient plant and so consider leaving a small patch to mine for nutrients in a damp area of your garden – harvest it twice a year for compost.

Shallow-rooted cultivated plants feed predominantly in the top 20cm of soil, so they will only be able to flourish when the soil is well tended, with plenty of organic matter incorporated where they need it. Deep-rooted plants raise plant foods from deep in the soil and make them available to shallow feeders. At the same time as they mine deep into the subsoil, they are opening up the soil, creating channels for aeration and water.

Don't be too hard on docks. They are not hard to pull or dig out when soil is slightly moist, and they do an excellent job of stabilising eroded or otherwise damaged soil. Their deep roots mine the subsoil for nutrients, while the large fleshy leaves yield large amounts of organic matter when they decay onto the soil. The related fat hen also makes calcium and iron available to other plants.

A garden full of nettles looks initially daunting, but nettles are busy bringing up numerous minerals and trace elements from the soil. Some of the most fertile soil in your garden will be where you have removed an established patch of nettles. Dandelions can become a bit of a pest, easy to remove from beds but troublesome in lawns and producing thousands of seeds. But they too are busy mining the soil for nutrients, bringing up significant quantities of iron, copper and potassium.

Comfrey can be an invasive weed in damp gardens, but it is a wonderful source of nutrients. The main roots of a comfrey plant can be 7cm diameter at the base, and will happily push 2m down in the soil to bring up large quantities of plant foods and trace elements. Never eradicate comfrey as it is one of the most useful plants in an organic garden, because of the number of nutrients it accumulates, and its speed of growth and decomposition (see page 20). Horsetail is also found in damp places, throwing up fruiting spores in spring followed by bristly upright stems. It is another greedy plant that brings to the surface whatever nutrients it can find.

WEEDS IN THE COMPOST

All weeds, even those with seriously aggressive root systems, can be composted. Dry invasive perennials first in the sun, or leave them to rot for several weeks in a black plastic sack before adding them to a heap.

Jerusalem artichokes – or cultivated vegetable sunflowers – quickly turn into aggressive weeds if they are not contained. They make an excellent addition to a compost heap, full of plant foods and fibre, but never add tubers to your heap as they will sprout and grow.

Woodash is high in potassium, but use sparingly in the garden as it is very alkaline. Keep woodash away from clay soils as it contains salts that can interfere with their structure and harm fertility.

Each time you weed your garden you remove the plants with all the nutrients they have robbed from the soil, plus new proteins and carbohydrates that they have manufactured. When you realise how many plant foods weeds can accumulate, you will want to use those nutrients to help other plants. Don't throw weeds out, instead spread them to dry on the soil where you have hoed or pulled them out, or compost them. Everything they have taken out of the soil can be returned to it, with interest, via your compost heap.

Compost heaps need to contain a balance of high-nitrogen and high-fibre materials. They also need regular additions of activators, materials high in nitrogen and other minerals to feed and stimulate the decomposing organisms. Nettles and other young green weeds are good activators because of their high levels of nitrogen. Don't worry about incorporating some annual weed seeds, you can weed them out later. Even the most invasive perennial weed roots such as ground elder will compost if they are thoroughly dried for a week or two in the sun, or well-rotted in a sealed plastic sack. Test they are not still alive by scattering some moist soil over them.

If you have abundant compost materials you can burn some perennial roots and scatter the bonfire ash in thin layers in your heap instead of lime. Woodash contains calcium, potassium and sodium, and shouldn't be used on heavy clay soils as it reacts with the clay and makes drainage problems even worse.

If there is no wild comfrey in your neighbourhood, you should grow it specially for the compost heap. Chop its roots into small pieces but its leaves and stems rot very swiftly, providing nutrients and feeding and speeding the processes at work in your compost. Comfrey is the organic gardener's main source of potassium to replenish the soil, containing two or three times as much as farmyard muck.

Compost tea is a useful pick-me-up for tired plants, and for plants growing in restricted soil in containers. Half fill a bucket with compost and cover it with water, leaving it to steep for 48 hours. Then dilute it to a pale amber colour and use fresh. Tea from compost made with quantities of horsetail makes a very effective fungicidal foliar feed or spray.

Bracken is an invasive weed in some areas, but an excellent addition to the compost heap, providing plenty of swift rotting bulk as well as plenty of plant foods. Chop it when it is green and still high in nutrients which diminish as it sets seed. Horsetail is another weed that composters should seek out. As well as secreting high levels of potassium and phosphorus, this ancient plant accumulates high levels of cobalt, calcium and silica which stimulate activity in a compost heap.

Several varieties of spurge are persistent annual weeds, irritating because some people are allergic to their milky sap. When they grow they rob the soil of boron, which is returned through composting. Sun spurge is most valuable as it steals most trace elements from the soil but all spurges help to maintain the temperature of a compost heap. Yarrow is another greedy plant, accumulating copper and useful amounts of phosphorus, potassium and calcium, which it gives up speedily into a compost heap.

It takes persistence to get rid of couch grass, but when you dig it up be sure it is destined for the compost heap. Its roots contain high levels of potassium, silica, chlorine and various trace elements which it steals from the ground as it grows. Dry roots for several weeks before chopping them up small and adding them to your compost heap. It is wise to replenish the ground where you have removed couch grass with compost containing the weed. This also seems to deter any couch rootlets that remain.

Deep-feeding weeds store considerable reserves of food in their roots so they are always valuable additions to compost. Spread dandelion, teasel and dock roots to dry before adding them. They are all more nutritious when they are young and must be cut for compost before they set seed.

WEEDS AS COMPANIONS

It used to be traditional practice to store apples on slatted trays lined with nettle leaves. This is reputed to keep the fruit from rotting.

Bad companions: Creeping buttercups and other members of the Ranunculaceae family make poor neighbours as the secretions from their roots poison nitrogen bacteria in the soil so that other plants suffer.

Valerian attracts insect friends, but fat hen and docks attract aphids. Chickweed attracts whitefly and red spider mite so should be cleared from glasshouses and tunnels in particular.

There are a number of ways that growing weeds can help cultivated plants, as long as they don't overwhelm them. In general, a good selection of weeds adds to the diversity of every organic garden, which everyone should aim for. The more varied your plants, the more diversity of insects, birds and animals, plus increased soil life – all adding up to a healthier garden.

Stinging nettles aren't popular additions to a garden border or vegetable bed, but leave a few round the edge of your vegetable beds. They host nettle aphids to feed early-waking ladybirds in spring. When they grow near tomatoes the fruits will ripen more quickly, and be less likely to rot; black, red and white currants will crop more heavily, herbs will produce more oils. Yarrow is another stimulant which helps neighbours to grow more strongly.

Some weeds like to grow hand-in-hand with cultivated plants – yields of wheat are actually improved by small numbers of corncockles, mayweed or white mustard. But crops are choked if weeds get out of hand, so they should be weeded out at crucial early stages of crop growth.

Plants with a wide leaf spread such as fat hen are useful in your vegetable bed, if kept under control. Their deep roots bring minerals to the soil surface and their wide leaf spread keeps the ground moist and shaded for seedlings. It can also be kept for use as a sacrificial plant as it attracts leafminers and aphids away from other plants.

Insect hotels

Sowthistle is a useful trap plant. It is host to leafminers and aphids, and should be left in the ground until early summer, then pulled up and composted – an efficient compost heap will kill pest and disease organisms. Clovers host beneficial insects, particularly predators of woolly aphis, so they are particularly useful left growing among apple trees. They also offer good cover for the ground beetles which prey on slugs and snails.

WEEDS AND WILDLIFE

A weed-free garden would be rather an unfriendly place for wildlife. Because weeds are such adaptable survivors, one or other is likely to be flowering at almost any time of year, providing food or nectar for animals and insects when there may be little choice. They may also help to keep wild creatures from eating your cultivated plants.

One of weeds' most important roles is to attract pest predators into your garden. Once you realise that nettles, nipplewort and even bindweed attract ladybirds and hoverflies, and therefore help keep aphids under control, you'll probably be happy to host a few. Similarly, ground beetles gravitate towards creeping thistle, ground elder and chickweed, from where they venture out to eat pest insects and even slugs and snails. Hoverflies are attracted to cow parsley. But a very tidy garden doesn't provide the support that these important predators need.

Ivy can be a nuisance, but leave some on walls or trees to provide shelter for birds, and butterflies will hibernate in its green depths. It also provides late autumn flowers for bees to build up stores of pollen for the winter. Ivy on the ground hosts many helpful beetles, and its deep cover makes a good hiding place for frogs and some useful small mammals.

Sowthistle attracts birds and insects, and this mineral-rich plant is an excellent addition to any animal's diet – vets use it to help problems with high blood pressure and heart disorders.

Groundsel is another valuable animal food – it was once grown as a crop to feed pigs, goats, rabbits and poultry, to add iron to their diet. In some European countries couch grass is still harvested specially for horse and cattle food, because it is so rich in minerals.

If you can keep them under control, blackberries are a favourite nectar plant for butterflies and make good cover for birds, as well as providing useful food.

EAT YOUR WEEDS

Weeds spread hand-in-hand with human activity, and humans have always found uses for the commonest ones. All medicines were originally made from wild plants, and weeds were often valued as food. When you are weeding your garden, save some for the pot – vegetables all developed from once-wild plants, and many weeds are very nutritious. Nettles are rich in vitamins A and C as well as minerals, and young leaves make a tasty as well as healthy soup. Dandelion leaves contain significant levels of vitamin A, vitamin C, several B vitamins, and many minerals including calcium, chlorine, copper, iron, phosphorus, potassium, magnesium, silicon and sulphur. Not bad for a weed! Eat young dandelion leaves in salads or pick the whole crown and blanch it for a minute in boiling water to take away any bitterness, then change the water and cook as spinach.

Fat hen is often cooked as a spinach-type vegetable, it contains more B vitamins and iron and protein than raw cabbage or spinach, and plenty of calcium. But always pick young plants as older ones store high levels of oxalic acid. If you don't manage to get rid of all your ground elder, brought to England by the Romans as a potherb, weaken what remains by regularly picking leaves for the pot – they taste quite pleasant with butter.

Salads

Wild sorrel is the same as cultivated, but it will be very acid if growing in acid soils, in which case use it as a cooked vegetable rather than as salad greens. Like fat hen, use only young leaves because it also contains oxalic acid. Chickweed was once sold on city streets as cress. It is a useful salad plant because it is one of the few herbs that contains significant amounts of copper, a trace element lacking in most of our diet. Hairy bittercress is another useful addition to the salad bowl and the leaves of garlic mustard add a pleasant garlic flavour.

HOW

DO I CONTROL THE WEEDS THAT I DON'T WANT?

Even the most persistent
weeds can be eradicated
with a bit of thought, hard
work and patience. Learn
how weeds operate and find
the most appropriate ways
to tackle them.

HOW DO WEEDS TAKE HOLD?

Chickweed, fat hen, dock and sowthistle host pest insects.

Groundsel, shepherd's purse and chickweed spread viral diseases. Charlock and shepherd's purse transmit club root.

The flowers and seeds of ragwort and corncockle are poisonous.

Groundsel and foxglove seedlings are poisonous – so be careful to remove them from salad beds where they could be mistakenly picked with a crop.

Weeds have their uses, but they also smother, choke and strangle cultivated plants. Some harbour pests and diseases, some are poisonous, and many spread fast and aggressively. While everyone should aim for diversity in their gardens, and should tolerate some weeds, gardeners rarely want to encourage them. You must find ways to prevent them arriving and spreading in your garden, and ways to remove those that are in residence, or arrive uninvited.

If you manage your soil well and build it up to be rich and fertile, you'll have few problems with weeds. But you'll never get rid of them altogether because they have evolved such efficient strategies for spreading. Understand how weeds survive and you'll give yourself the best chance of controlling them.

Seeds

All garden soil has a huge seed bank of weed seeds, some dormant, some ready to germinate. Weeds are survivors, and plants often produce vast quantities of seeds – one fat hen plant can drop around half a million seeds in a good year. All annual and some perennial weeds spread by seed, so you should always try and remove them before they flower and set seed. But hundreds of thousands more will blow in, or arrive on passing animals, carried by birds, on the soles of your shoes, or brought by visitors.

Some seeds are designed to travel, others to stay put, depending which serves their purposes. Coltsfoot, nipplewort and many others have tiny seeds that blow about easily. Dandelion, groundsel and thistle seeds blow about with the help of tiny parachutes. Willowherbs have hairs to catch the wind, weed trees such as sycamore have winged seeds like helicopters. Blackberry seeds need to travel so plants can colonise new areas, and they germinate most easily after passing through a bird's gut.

Cleavers and burdock seeds have velcro-like hooks to grab on to passing animals' coats. Shepherd's purse seeds, oxalis and Himalayan balsam shoot out of their seed pods at the slightest touch, and are often inadvertently spread through weeding.

Roots, runners and rhizomes

Hardy perennial weeds do produce seeds, but these are often just for back-up as they spread vegetatively. Weeds with tap roots have a large simple or branched storage root. A new plant will grow from even the tiniest piece of root left in the ground or cut up when you are digging or cultivating the ground. Some of the most invasive weeds, including couch grass and ground elder also spread from segments of root. Additionally, they have long branching rhizomes or roots under the ground so they can spread over 8-10 sq. metres in one season.

Bindweed spreads rampantly above ground, strangling other plants that it uses as support. With other aggressive weeds including coltsfoot it grows equally rampantly beneath the surface, sending down deep-spreading roots that regrow whenever top sections are removed. One root of bindweed can develop over one season into a network reaching a terrifying 25 sq. metres. Horsetail is almost as active. Creeping buttercup and wild strawberry run along the ground, producing plantlets at regular intervals which put down roots and send out more runners. Blackberries can shoot 1m a week in summer, sending stem roots into the ground to develop into more plants.

Control

The best line of attack is always prevention, and good soil management will control weeds in time. Even persistent problems such as horsetail will disappear as soil becomes more fertile. Cultivate carefully; time spent in eradicating weeds when they first appear is time well spent.

Perennial spreaders

- *Tap roots (and seed)*
  Comfrey *Symphytum officinale*
  Cow parsley *Anthriscus sylvestris*
  Dandelion *Taraxacum officinale*
  Dock *Rumex spp.*
  Teasel *Dipsacus fullonum*
- *Runners above ground*
  Blackberry *Rubus fruticosa*
  Creeping buttercup *Ranunculus repens*
  Creeping cinquefoil *Potentilla reptans*
  Ground ivy *Glechoma hederacea*
  Selfheal *Prunella vulgaris*
  Silverweed *Potentilla anserina*
  Wild strawberry *Fragaria vesca*
- *Shallow-running roots*
  Couch grass *Agropyron repens*
  Ground elder *Aegopodium podagraria*
  Nettle *Urtica dioica*
  Rosebay willowherb *Epilobium angustifolium*
- *Deep-spreading roots*
  Bindweed *Convolvulus arvensis*
  Coltsfoot *Tussilago farfara*
  Creeping thistle *Cirsium arvense*
  Hedge bindweed *Calystegia sepium*
  Horsetail *Equisetum arvensis*
  Ivy *Hedera helix*
- *Corms or bulbils*
  Lesser celandine *Ranunculus ficaria*
  Oxalis *Oxalis articulata*

DIGGING AND ROTOVATING

Night time cultivation

As seeds need light to germinate, research suggests that cultivating and weeding at night may reduce weed problems. This may reduce germination of a few varieties, but most weed seeds in the top centimetre of soil still receive enough light to germinate.

Rotovating means that you can't plant that area of your garden for a season as it takes several months to clear a very weedy plot. Don't try and rotovate until your soil is dry and warm in spring because rotovating a cold winter-wet soil will do long-term damage to its structure.

If your ground is full of perennial weeds that flourish in poorer conditions (see pages 12-15) it suggests that your soil needs a lot of work to bring it up to the state where most cultivated plants will flourish. In this case it's a good idea to double dig the ground before you plant.

Double digging

This involves turning over the subsoil as well as the top-soil, adding organic matter to each. The only rule is not to mix the levels of subsoil and topsoil. The best way is to divide the plot to be dug into roughly 45cm squares. Take out a spit of topsoil from the first and second squares and a spit of subsoil from the first square, and leave these to one side. Then take the subsoil from the second square and turn it into the first square, adding compost or manure with it. Cover this with weeded topsoil from the third square, also mixed with organic matter, and so on. The topsoil and subsoil from your starting point ends up in the final square.

Clearing by rotovating

An alternative tactic is to use a rotovator, a powered digger with tines that chop up the surface layers of soil, and any weeds it contains. But you must rotovate very weedy ground several times to clear it as each time you rotovate you will chop up weed roots and potentially spread any that are left in the ground. For best results you need to go over the ground once a month in dry weather between April and July. This will gradually destroy the foliage the new rootlets send up, and weaken them to death.

Only ever rotovate soil when it is dry, or you spread weeds further. Always add generous quantities of organic matter to the soil as you clear it, as even in the best conditions rotovating will harm the soil structure. You should also mulch well with organic material after rotovating to help restore the soil's structure.

HOEING AND HANDWEEDING

Regular weeding is the way to success, but it is better to handweed as often as you can rather than excessive hoeing, as this can damage the soil's structure. Light hoeing once every two or three weeks is plenty, but you can handweed whenever you like.

Hoes are most useful where you can weed between straight lines of vegetables, so mark your rows with string before you sow. If young seedlings are out of line they risk being beheaded with the weeds when you hoe.

The most critical period of weed control is the four weeks following germination of your planted seeds. After that, weeds can still interfere with your plants. They may look unsightly and can harbour unwanted pests and diseases, but your plants will have a good chance of surviving any competition. So if you only manage to keep weeds under control for that critical time from late spring to early summer, you'll have gone a long way to help the productivity in your garden.

Handweeding and hoeing

The most useful tools for weed control are a handfork and a hoe. A hoe cuts weeds off from their roots just below the soil surface, and is most useful for keeping the ground clear between rows of plants.

Small weeds and larger annuals can be pulled out by hand, using a handfork to help you ease the plant out where necessary. Follow an old adage and 'pull when wet, hoe when dry'. If you try and pull weeds out by hand when the soil is very dry, the roots will simply break off and remain in the ground. In wet soil you can pull up even long taproots without difficulty, and without major disturbance to the ground.

Regular hoeing is a good way of keeping beds clear of all but heavy weed growth. But you need dry weather for hoeing so that every weed you dislodge will die straight away and so that the weeds you leave on the surface will shrivel and die fast.

Several types of hoe exist and gardeners usually develop personal preferences. A Dutch hoe, sometimes called a push hoe, has a blade which is sharp on the lower edge, and a two-edged hoe is sharpened on both edges. These have a gap between the blade and the handle so that weeds and soil pass over the hoe's blade as you move it backwards and forwards just beneath the surface of the soil, chopping off any plants it meets. The blade of a draw hoe is attached directly to the handle, and this is used on the soil's surface to chop off larger weeds. You can also purchase short-handled draw hoes, sometimes called onion hoes, for weeding in small areas.

Chopping down perennial weeds

You need to get your timing right to be successful in the war against perennials. They depend on stores of food in their large roots or tubers, and if you hoe them off in spring the roots will simply regenerate. It is best to smother them or dig them out, or hit strong weeds with the hoe when they are weakest – when they're just about to flower. Then their food reserves are at their lowest.

Spade or fork?

Only use a spade for initial ground clearance. It is counter-productive to try and dig out weeds with long runners and rhizomes that appear in the middle of cultivated plants. Every tiny bit of root that remains in the ground will grow into another plant. You must pull them out carefully, using hands and a handfork, or a fork if the problem is sizeable. If weed roots are tangled around established plants, you will need to remove those plants and disentangle any runners from their roots before replanting.

Flame weeding

Flame weeding can be useful for removing weeds in some places, such as on stony paths and walls where you can't hoe and weeds won't budge with handweeding. You don't burn the weeds to a crisp – just pass a flame over them until they change to a darker green which shows that their cells walls have burst. But flame weeding is slow. You may need to keep attacking the weeds every few days for a week or two. And it is costly – you must buy a propri-etary flame weeder, never make your own.

Always be careful with gifts of plants from friends' and neighbours' gardens. Check the roots of the plants very carefuly and remove any hints of runners or rhizomes before planting them.

SOWING TO AVOID COMPETITION

Weeds are designed to survive. It is estimated that 25 per cent of all weed seeds will germinate 10 years after being buried in the soil at depths below 2m. Some will remain viable for centuries.

Wherever possible, sow seeds into 'plugs' or 'modules' that decompose, so you place the pot straight into the soil. Recycle cardboard egg boxes, use tubes of newspaper twisted at the base, or buy compressed coir or paper pots.

Even when you seem to have cleared the worst of your weeds, your soil will still hold a huge store of weed seeds, waiting for the right conditions to germinate.

Fooling weed seeds

When you prepare a seed bed for your cultivated vegetables and annual flowers, you are also creating perfect conditions for many weed seeds. You can sow your chosen seed very thickly, to compete aggressively with weed seeds, thinning out your plants later. But a better way is to cheat weeds into getting going before your chosen seeds. This is ideal in soils that warm up early in spring.

The trick is to prepare your seed bed two weeks earlier than you want to plant your first seeds. Cover it with clear plastic or horticultural fleece to warm the ground. A first flush of annual weeds will take advantage of the conditions, and will quickly germinate and sprout. Leave this 'stale seed bed' for two weeks, when most seeds will have sprouted. Then hoe them off, leave their decaying remains as a nitrogen-rich mulch, and sow your seeds as usual. This technique won't get rid of all your weeds, but it will remove most competition from your chosen plants when they are most vulnerable.

Giving seeds a headstart

You can only prepare a stale seed bed in warm soils, as cold soils can't be worked until too late in spring to allow two weeks grace for weeds. The best way to avoid weed competition in heavier soils is to sow seeds into modules or small containers. Then plant them out when they are strong enough to outgrow any weeds, and when you have had the chance to hoe or pull out early starters. It is also much easier to remove weeds around recognisable seedlings than around small sprouts. Use biodegradeable containers where possible to avoid disturbing the roots of young seedlings.

PLANTING TO OUTWIT WEEDS

Try to stagger your planting through the seasons so you can keep up with any weeding that does need attending to. Even if you're not growing winter vegetables, crops such as garlic can be planted in autumn to get established over winter and early spring before weeds take hold. Perennial vegetables such as Swiss chard stay in the ground over the winter to give an early crop from established plants.

Plant leafy vegetables in blocks, rather than rows, to smother small weeds.

You can plant ground-cover plants to prevent weeds emerging. But be careful what you choose. Many ground-cover plants such as periwinkles (*Vinca spp.*) or St John's Wort (*Hypericum perforatum*) can themselves become invasive weeds.

Don't be put off gardening because you haven't the time or energy to clear all your weeds before you plant, sometimes you may have to find other ways to manage a weedy plot. While some plants are very susceptible to competition, others will survive and even flourish.

Choosing varieties

If you're worried that you may have a weed problem, and you haven't started seedlings in modules, first concentrate on large-seeded vegetables such as beans, sunflowers and squash, which need minimal weeding and are strong enough to rise above most annual weeds. Those with large spreading leaves additionally shade the soil so that weed seedlings are deprived of light.

The stronger the cultivated plant variety, the better it will compete with weeds. So choose hardy bushy or climbing varieties of beans and tomatoes, and high-yielding vigorous varieties of other crops.

Cut-and-come-again salad plants mean that the ground is covered with mature plants for many weeks. The less bare soil in your garden, the less room for weeds to move in.

Intercropping

Take advantage of the way plants grow at different rates to sow fast-growing ones around slower ones. That way you can use the same space for two crops or more in one season, and keep the ground constantly covered so weeds can't get a foothold. Sow radishes, for example, in spring between other salads. Sow fast-growing leafy lettuces around slender-leaved slow-growing garlic and onions. Use fast-growing brassicas such as rocket and mustards around peas and beans.

Use annuals as fillers in herbaceous borders. Sow seeds thickly and later thin them out if necessary, creating an attractive living weed-suppressing mulch.

SMOTHERING WEEDS

Always mulch soil when it is warm and moist but not wet. Too wet and the mulch prevents it drying out so the ground gets waterlogged; too dry and the mulch may prevent it ever getting wet enough as moisture filters slowly through a mulch.

Never use hay as a weed suppressing mulch as it often brings thousands of weed seeds with it.

Use beech or oak leaves; or even pine needles to suppress weeds on strawberry beds, as strawberries like the acid conditions this creates. If organic mulch is not well-rotted, you must rake it off before cultivation as it will take a population explosion of bacteria in the soil to decompose and incorporate it, and they will use up available nitrogen for their own development, causing a shortage in the soil. Well-rotted matter is easily assimilated.

You may not always be able, or want, to cultivate to get weeds under control – if time is limited, if you have a large scale problem, or if you are prepared to wait. As almost all plants need light to grow, a good way to keep weeds at bay is to mulch your ground well with sheet mulches – mulches that completely cover the ground. These are ideal for suppressing weeds where you don't mind waiting to have useable ground, or in order to keep things under control in one area while you concentrate on another. Mulches should also be used around plants in established beds to discourage weeds.

At the same time as controlling weeds, mulches improve your soil's structure by preventing erosion, keeping the ground moist and warm. And organic mulches add plant food. Always mulch moist soil.

Biodegradeable mulches

If you have large supplies of garden compost, well-rotted manure or organic mushroom compost then these make effective soil-improving and weed-suppressing mulches. Lay them over several sheets of overlapping newsprint or thin cardboard for best effect.

Autumn leaves are easy for most gardeners to get hold of. Store them in bins for a year to rot into leafmould or run a lawnmower over them to shred them finely before applying a 10-15cm layer as a mulch. Grass clippings make a good mulch at any time of year as long as they are not too wet – you can use them to keep weeds down in cultivated beds, or as sheet mulches. Half-rotted straw is another good sheet mulch, but don't use hay as it often contains millions of annual weed seeds.

Woodchips and forest bark can make an attractive mulch, but only use them well-composted as they can contain toxins from the forestry processes. Either use them around established plants, or over a sheet mulch of well-rotted compost or manure. Like sawdust, they must be left to decay for six months to a year or they can tie up soil nitrogen.

Organic mulches are best for annual weeds. Simply pull out any weeds that do get through and replenish mulches as they are incorporated into the soil. Persistent perennial weeds may work their way up through the mulches so you may need to control these with other materials. Old natural woollen carpet makes an effective barrier and light excluder, and it can be left to decompose as wool is high in nutrients.

Inorganic mulches

If you inherit a garden full of really persistent weeds, long-term mulching is often the best solution, as you will need to clear any existing infested areas completely.

Then your best bet is to choose black plastic mulch, which is available in several thicknesses. Always purchase the thickest grade you can afford as thin plastic will only last one season and you will need to leave a mulch down for two or more seasons to solve really bad infestations. Nonporous black plastic smothers soil organisms along with the weeds, so there will be a lot of work to do when you lift the mulch. It's a better investment all round to buy porous horticultural plastic. This woven material stops weeds effectively, but allows air and water through and doesn't disable soil life. You can use it to smother even badly infested areas for one season. Then plant shrubs, trees, perennials and most vegetable seedlings through it the following year, and either harvest through the plastic or remove it and replace it if necessary.

Always improve soil properly before laying a woven plastic mulch. Once the mulch is in place it's hard to get at the soil to replenish soil life.

Use black plastic mulches to clear land and eradicate stubborn perennial weeds. Once you have cleared the plot, you can re-lay porous mulches and plant through them, or use them as mats around fruit trees and shrubs.

All sheet mulches must be firmly pegged with stakes or weighted down with stones.

ANTI-WEED MULCHES — CHECKLISTS

Annual weed problems
- compost
- muck
- straw
- autumn leaves
- grass mowings
- mushroom compost
- newspaper with any of the above

Compost and well-rotted muck
Provides food, improves soil life. Use on vegetable beds and around perennial plantings.

Straw
Use partially rotted straw on perennial beds . Don't use in vegetable beds as it may cause nitrogen robbery.

Autumn leaves
Use leafmould as anti-weed and conditioning mulch anywhere in the garden. Or shredded leaves around permanent plantings.

Mushroom compost
Obtain from an organic source, or compost for six months before using on vegetable and permanent beds.

Newspaper
Only use black and white newsprint. Spread around six pages thick and use as an addition to organic mulches.

Grass mowings

Use 10cm layers of rotted grass clippings or 5cm layers of fresh clippings around annuals and perennials. Be careful they don't heat up too much.

Flattened cardboard boxes

An alternative to plastic against perennial weeds.

Bark and sawdust

Make sure they are well-composted to remove toxins.

Carpet

Use old hessian-backed woollen carpet against perennial weeds.

Black plastic

Use to clear badly infested land. Woven porous plastic is a useful mulch for permanent plantings.

Perennial problems

- thick carpet
- black plastic
- cardboard with organic matter

Maintenance

- top up levels of organic mulch regularly, pulling out any weeds that appear
- place porous plastic mats around trees and shrubs in grassland and orchards

RAISED BEDS AND BARRIERS

Advantages of raised beds
- Manageable size, so easy to work and keep weeds under control
- No digging required, so the weed seedbank can't germinate
- High fertility – good structure and ideal conditions for cultivated plants
- Easy to maintain fertility – just top up with compost or well-rotted organic matter regularly
- Depth of soil means you can plant closer together for increased productivity
- Loose deep soil means it is easy to pull out any weeds that do appear

If you're faced with a very weedy garden, and you want to get growing quickly, one alternative is to build raised beds. Even raising a bed 15cm above ground level can help control weeds.

Mark out beds no wider than two arms' reach in breadth for ease of working, and edge them with material of your choice, depending on the height you wish to build them. Wooden planks are fine for shallow raised beds. Whatever materials you use for higher beds, make sure they are strong enough to contain the volume of soil.

You need to double dig the ground before constructing shallow raised beds (see page 34), or at least aerate the subsoil thoroughly with a fork. If you raise the beds 30cm or more above the ground you don't even need to dig the ground first. Just chop down weeds and build beds straight over a thick layer of compost laid on the soil. Then add well-rotted manure, compost and topsoil. If you have to bring in topsoil, watch out for its quality as it may be very dusty or sticky and is often full of new weed seeds. Ideally, make raised beds in autumn and sheet-mulch with cardboard covered with a layer of organic matter, then plant through this in spring.

The growing medium in raised beds will be loose and friable so that perennial weeds can easily be pulled out if they appear among your plants. You should never need to dig raised beds, just top up with compost, so you'll never expose waiting weed seeds to the light they need to germinate and grow.

Barriers
If your garden has a perennial weed problem, chances are that your neighbours will have one as well. To avoid weeds spreading, clear them from the edges of your property and dig a trench about 45cm deep and 15cm wide at any boundary or beneath a dividing fence. Line it with heavyduty polythene, or bricks, slates or tiles.

SOIL STRATEGIES — ROTATION

A traditional system rotates potatoes, brassicas, legumes and roots on a four-year cycle, but you don't need to follow this slavishly. As long as you don't grow the same crop year after year in the same place, you should have few problems.

If clovers, vetches or medick seed themselves in your vegetable garden, leave a patch as green manure as part of your rotation.

If you manage your soil well you should have few weed problems, and once your garden is established you will scarcely need to weed. Maintain high levels of organic matter in your soil, keep an eye on drainage, and test the pH regularly to ensure you give your plants the best chances by growing them in the conditions they prefer. Plants struggle if conditions don't suit them, and weak stressed plants are easily undermined by competition.

Rotation

Practising rotation in a vegetable bed helps keep your soil healthy, and therefore prevents weeds from getting established as well as deterring pests and diseases.

If you grow one species continually this can exhaust the soil of a particular range of nutrients, then cultivated plants begin to struggle and opportunist weeds jump in. When you change crops each year you maintain fertility so weeds have less chance to get established.

Potatoes have always been used as ground clearers, and other greedy feeders such as squash also leave the ground fairly weed-free for other crops to follow. They additionally suppress weeds because of their generous leaf spread, so you can follow them with crops that are more susceptible to weeds such as peas and beans.

Another advantage of rotation is that your garden will be divided into manageable sections. So if a weed problem does occur, it is likely to be concentrated in a small area of your garden, within one type of crop, rather than throughout. You can then solve it by cultivating or mulching that particular area, or sowing a green manure to rebuild the soil's fertility and crowd out weeds. This still leaves most of your garden available for planting. Rotation also means that planting will be staggered throughout the year, or at least over the spring and summer, so you should always be able to keep on top of any problems that do occur.

BAD COMPANIONS

If you use tomatoes to clear an infestation of couch grass, don't cultivate potatoes or tomatoes the following year, otherwise you risk the build-up of pests or diseases in the soil.

Some weeds inhibit the growth of cultivated plants by excreting substances in their roots or flowers. Fat hen, for example, releases toxic levels of oxalic acid into the soil when it starts flowering, to inhibit the growth of any neighbouring plants. Creeping buttercups and others release substances that poison nitrogen bacteria in the soil so other plants become deficient.

Fortunately, some cultivated plants have similar effects on weeds.

Tomatoes and marigolds

Plant tomatoes in areas of your garden troubled by couch grass. Use them as sacrificial plants even where you can't expect to harvest the fruits, as their root excretions can deter vigorous infestations of the weed. Simply turn the couch-ridden area over to one spade's depth in early summer, throw some good topsoil or planting compost between the upturned clods and heel in young tomato plants – use a vigorous variety such as Broad Yellow ripple currant which itself grows wild as a weed in some areas of the southern United States. Compost the tomato plants in autumn and mulch the ground over winter. The following season your ground should be couch-free.

The African marigold (*Tagetes minuta*) seems also to excrete powerful herbicides from its roots. Start seeds indoors to be sure of successful germination, and plant strong seedlings into ground infested with persistent perennial weeds such as bindweed, ground elder and horsetail. Provided the young plants get established, they should suppress all but the most serious infestation. Marigolds only seem to have an effect on plants with starchy roots, so they can be safely planted near woody rooted plants such as shrubs, roses and soft fruit. Keep them out of herbaceous borders and only plant them round the edge of vegetable beds or they may inhibit or even destroy some plants you want, along with weeds.

WEEDS IN PATHS AND WALLS

Use an old kitchen knife to weed between bricks and slabs, slipping the blade down to chop weeds as near the roots as possible. Or take hold of the top of the weed firmly and pull very gently to ease it out; never let weeds in paths flower and set seed.

If an old brick or paved path is very hard to keep weed-free, sow annual flower seeds in any gaps to compete with the weeds.

Paths in vegetable beds

Pathways covered in an organic material such as bark chippings are ideal for a vegetable garden, and are easy to maintain – if they get weedy hoe them or dig them in and start again. But don't use old hay as it contains weed seeds and can aggravate problems.

You should never need to waste time weeding where you walk – a path that takes a lot of foot traffic rarely has a chance to get weedy, so a weedy path may mean you don't really need a path at all. Stepping stones through a border may serve as well, or turn a weedy path through lawn back into grass, insetting some slabs if you wish. Slabs in grass must be at ground level for easy mowing.

Whatever path you choose, make sure it is laid well – concrete , slabs and pavers are then very resistant to weeds. Paths made of old bricks or slabs are attractive, but it can be hard to uproot weeds by hand so if they get very weedy you should either repeatedly flame weed (see page 37), or preferably lift and relay them. Dig the path out to at least 20cm below ground level, fill the bottom 8cm with gravel and cover this with a thick layer of sand under the bricks or slabs. This prevents weeds from seeding and rooting and provides drainage. Then brush a dry mix of sand and cement into cracks between paving slabs so weeds can't develop.

Gravel paths are easier to weed – you can use a hoe in severe cases, or handweed. You can scatter seeds of attractive ornamentals on gravel, or plant some herbs. If you want a plant-free path, spread a layer of porous plastic (see page 43) at the bottom of the 20cm trench then fill with gravel. Edge paths with wood or vertical stones to avoid grass and weeds spreading from lawns or borders.

Weedy walls

If dry stone walls get really covered in ivy or full of creeping perennial weeds you ought to take them apart and rebuild them if at all possible. But weeds such as creeping Jenny and herb Robert look attractive clambering out of walls, and most annuals can be easily pulled out without harming the wall. Ivy is fine climbing strong walls, but it delights in pushing into weak and crumbling mortar and can damage or destroy weak walls so pull it out carefully.

WEEDY LAWNS

Common lawn weeds
Dandelion *Taraxacum officinale*
Plantain *Plantago major*
Daisy *Bellis perennis*
Hawkweed *Hieracium spp.*
Yarrow *Achillea millefolium*
Cat's ear *Hypochaeris radicata*

Soil pH is crucial to a healthy lawn, which depends on earthworm activity to drag down any rotting matter and prevent build-up of thatch. Earthworms will not survive if the pH is below 5.5.

Topdressing keeps a lawn in good condition and therefore discourages weeds. In early autumn scatter onto the lawn a mixture of compost and topsoil – finely worked molehill soil is perfect. This improves the surface structure and encourages earthworms.

Grass needs the right conditions for healthy growth just like other cultivated plants, so a weedy lawn probably means a problem with your soil. If you inherit a thoroughly weedy lawn it is best to remove the turf, stack it to rot into loam, and improve the soil before resowing. Remove weeds, check the pH of the soil and add lime if it is at all acid. Then dig in plenty of compost or organic matter to improve structure and fertility, with extra topsoil if necesary to build up the soil level. Prepare a seed bed and resow, choosing a suitable grass seed mixture – meadow grasses grow in the shade, rye grass is hard wearing.

If resowing is not an option, handweed plantains, dandelions and any other weeds with large flat leaves that smother the grass. Remove creeping buttercups as they suppress the growth of grass and clovers. Ease lawn weeds out carefully with an old kitchen knife or very fine trowel. Sprinkle finely ground lime or powdered seaweed if pH is acid. Encourage healthy growth with regularly mowing, leaving clippings on the grass to feed the lawn and encourage earthworm activity.

Weeds will do better than grass in very wet or very dry areas, so keep your lawn well-drained and moss-free by raking out patches of thatch, and aerate compacted areas regularly by spiking them with your garden fork.

Helpful weeds
Some weeds can be encouraged to keep your lawn healthy – and attractive. Clovers maintain nitrogen levels, helping grass to stay lush and green; yarrow stays dark green in the driest weather; and creeping wild thyme (*Thymus serpyllum*) also withstands drought and has a beautiful scent. Daisies, bird's-foot trefoil and other wildflowers add interesting leaf shapes as well as flowers if you let them. The more you mow, the better the texture of your lawn becomes as weeds produce smaller and smaller leaves to become increasingly dense.

GARDEN FRIENDS OR FOES?

Restrictions

Except in a very large garden, never plant mints (*Mentha spp.*) or horseradish (*Armoracia rusticana*) in an open bed. Instead, grow them in buried containers.

Ground cover

Be careful when choosing ornamental plants for ground cover. Their nature is to cover ground quickly and effectively, and virtually any ground-cover plant can become an invasive nuisance.

Think hard before you invite some plants into your garden as they can become invasive weeds in the garden and beyond. Japanese knotweed (*Polygonum cuspidatum*) was once a valued garden plant; it escaped and became so invasive that it is now illegal to plant it deliberately.

Borage has become a weed in many British gardens, but fortunately it is easy to control by removing flower-heads before they seed; its perennial relative green alkanet (*Pentaglottis sempervirens*) spreads fast via seed and roots and has a deep tap root which regenerates itself if it is broken, so every shred needs to be removed. Fortunately alkanet is fast decomposing and full of minerals, so it is a useful compost weed. Goldenrod (*Solidago officinalis*) can easily become another perennial pest with its aggressive root system and invasive habit – and it produces thousands of seeds. Keep its growth under check by dividing it each year and removing unwanted seedlings.

Tansy (*Tanacetum vulgaris*) is useful for attracting beneficial insects, and it may repel harmful ones, but its strong growth and huge seed production means it will speedily crowd out other plants very quickly. It is a helpful plant, but ideally you should grow it in containers so you can move it round the garden so other plants can enjoy its companion qualities without being devoured by it.

Jerusalem artichokes (*Helianthus tuberosus*) are vigorous perennial sunflowers with sprouting edible roots. They are valuable food plants, and their height (to 3m) means they can also be planted as useful weather shields, but keep their growing area contained by digging out all roots outside a chosen patch in late autumn. Never dig over a dormant patch of roots or you'll spread them everywhere.

If you buy wild strawberry plants (*Fragaria vesca*) be sure to get a named variety, otherwise your beds and lawn can quickly be taken over by this little creeping plant which produces thousands of offsets and no fruits.

DON'T WORRY ABOUT WEEDS

Every garden will have weeds, but they don't have to be a problem. Of course it's ideal to spend time maintaining and enjoying your garden as often as you can throughout the year, but you may not always have the right amount of time at the right season. Even when you can't do as much as you might like, you can make sure your garden doesn't get overwhelmed by weeds, and you don't get overwhelmed by your garden.

Your garden is not a battleground

Make your garden the right size for you – the more space you cultivate, the more space for weeds, and the more difficult it is to keep on top of everything. And don't be impatient – never sow seeds or plant seedlings too early in spring or they will be subdued by competition from weeds that can happily cope with the conditions better than your chosen plants.

A good gardener must learn to relax – if you only have limited time to garden, and this coincides with wet or foul weather, do something else instead. It very rarely matters if you plant something later than it says on the packet or the pot. But you can make matters very hard for yourself if you try to cultivate your soil when it is too wet or too dry, and when your soil is stressed weeds can move in wholesale. Be generous with yourself and seed heavily if you fear a huge crop of annual weeds germinating along with your chosen seeds – you can thin your plants later when danger of competition has passed. Then, if you can, take time to weed in spring and early summer when your young plants are developing. If you can't get at weeds later in the season, it doesn't matter much as they will pose less threat to your plants.

And finally, learn to love your weeds. Eat them, compost them or just appreciate them – once you think of hedge bindweed as white morning glory it can even seem beautiful!

FOLESHILL

RESOURCES

Organisations to join
Centre for Alternative Technology (CAT)
Machynlleth
Powys SY20 9AZ
01654 702400
info@cat.org.uk

HDRA, the organic organisation
Ryton Gardens
Ryton on Dunsmore
Coventry
Warwickshire CV8 3LG
024 7630 3517
enquiry@hdra.org.uk

Soil Association
Bristol House
40-56 Victoria Street
Bristol BS1 6BY
0117 929 0661
info@soilassociation.org

Mail order
Chase Organics
Riverdene Business Park
Molesey Road
Horsham
Surrey KT12 4RG
01932 253666
www.OrganicCatalog.com
suppliers of seeds, tools and equipment

Gardening on the web
Centre for Alternative Technology (CAT)
www.cat.org.uk

HDRA, the organic organisation
www.hdra.org.uk

Organic UK
www.organic.mcmail.com

Soil Association
www.soilassociation.org

More books to read
Peter Harper, *Natural Garden Book*, Gaia Books, 1994

Audrey Wynne Hatfield, *How to enjoy your weeds*, Plum Tree publishing, 1998

Pauline Pears and Sue Stickland, *RHS Organic Gardening*, Octopus, 1995

Jo Readman, *Weeds, how to control and love them*, HDRA/Search Press, 1991

John Seymour, *The Complete Book of Self Sufficiency*, Dorling Kindersley, 1997

INDEX

A GAIA ORIGINAL

Books from Gaia celebrate the vision of Gaia, the self-
sustaining living Earth, and seek to help its readers live
in greater personal and planetary harmony.

Design	Lucy Guenot, Mark Epton
Editor	Pip Morgan
Index	Mary Warren
Photography	Steve Teague
Production	Lyn Kirby
Direction	Joss Pearson, Patrick Nugent

First published in the United Kingdom in 2001 by
Gaia Books Ltd, 66 Charlotte Street, London W1T 4QE
and 20 High Street, Stroud, Gloucestershire GL5 1AZ

ISBN 1 85675 132 5

A catalogue record of this book is available from the British
Library.

Printed and bound in Singapore by Kyodo

10 9 8 7 6 5 4 3 2 1

The Edible Container Garden

Michael Guerra ISBN 1 85675 089 2 £11.99
Plan well, plant properly and care for your soil for maximum produce from minimum space.

A Heritage of Flowers

Tovah Martin ISBN 1 85675 093 0 £14.99
This book tells of the history of old-fashioned flowers, both garden and wild, and the importance of their continued survival.

Heritage Vegetables

Sue Stickland ISBN 1 85675 033 7 £14.99
A guide to collecting, exchanging and cultivating old-fashioned vegetable seeds, and why you should choose to grow them.

G is for ecoGarden

Nigel Dudley and Sue Stickland ISBN 1 85675 035 3 £4.99
This handy A-Z guide provides information about everything ecological for your garden, from compost bins to attractant plants.

The Rothschild Gardens

Miriam Rothschild et al ISBN 1 85675 112 0 £16.99
Wildflower meadows, parks and gardens created by the Rothschilds. Photography by Andrew Lawson.

To order a book or request a catalogue contact:
Gaia Books Ltd, 20 High Street, Stroud, Glos GL5 1AZ
T: 01453 752985 F: 01453 752987 E: info@gaiabooks.co.uk

visit our web site to see a complete list of our titles: www.gaiabooks.co.uk